making Love a way of life

Argus Communications, Niles, Illinois

Printed in the United States of America.

Argus Communications
7440 Natchez Ave.
Niles, Illinois 60648

International Standard Book Number: 0-913592-84-6
Library of Congress Number: 76-54490

3 4 5 6 7 8 9 0

WRITTEN BY
DAVE MARQUIS

ILLUSTRATED BY
PAIGE THOMPSON

On Being A Great Lover

A "How To" Book of
Joyous Suggestions

Some of these suggestions
will apply to anyone, some to
special people in your life.

Do not read this book too fast. It has aged
twenty four years in preparation. Like good
wine, it is best when sipped.

THE WORDS
IN THIS BOOK
ARE DEDICATED TO
PAIGE THOMPSON.

THE ILLUSTRATIONS
IN THIS BOOK
ARE DEDICATED TO
DAVE MARQUIS.

WHY A LOVER?

YOU, AS A LOVER, LIKE HOW YOUR LOVE MAKES YOU FEEL, HOW IT MAKES OTHERS FEEL, AND BECAUSE THE MORE YOU GIVE, THE MORE YOU HAVE.

BUT YOU DON'T LOVE JUST TO BE LOVED. THAT IS INCIDENTAL. YOU LOVE BECAUSE YOU, LIKE ALL PEOPLE, ARE A BORN LOVER. THIS IS THE ONE THING THAT WE ALL HAVE IN COMMON. BUT SADLY, MOST PEOPLE JUST DON'T KNOW HOW OR NEVER GET STARTED OR THOUGHT THEY BETTER NOT, AND SO THEY NEVER KNOW THE WONDERS OF THEIR OWN LOVE.

BUT YOU, LOVER, FOUND OUT ABOUT LOVING, YOU WERE LOVED, AND YOU LIKED IT, YOU LOVED IN RETURN, AND YOU HAVE BEEN LOVING EVER SINCE.

THIS BOOK IS TO HELP YOU BECOME THE LOVER YOU WERE BORN TO BE.

Preface

We know love is of the heart, of the body, too, but when it came to loving, the mind was left out, which is sad. With the mind we can think of ways to love others, create ways to express our love, and maybe, if we are unafraid, find out how much love we are capable of.

Someday we will reach the farthest planet, run the fastest race, and cure the common cold, and then we will turn to each other and say, "What next?" And the answer will be, "We are" because the human frontier will be the last one, and we will have no choice but to explore it.

Or perhaps we will face the end of ourselves in the wars of famine, the exhaustion of our resources, and then we will avert our eyes from the swollen belly of hunger and turn to see each other. And we will recognize our common mortal dilemma

AND TRY FURIOUSLY TO LOVE EACH OTHER BEFORE IT IS OVER.

OR WE MAY BEGIN NOW OUR SEARCH TO DISCOVER OUR OWN, AND THEREIN THE WORLD'S, POTENTIAL FOR LOVE. WE ALREADY KNOW THAT LOVE MAKES US FEEL SECURE, FULFILLED, AND WARM. BUT GOING BEYOND THAT SLIGHT, YET COMFORTING, BIT OF KNOWLEDGE REQUIRES THOUGHT AND APPLICATION, EXPERIMENTATION AND EFFORT. IT REQUIRES RECOGNIZING THAT LOVING IS AN ABILITY, A CONSCIOUSLY DEVELOPED, SKILLED WAY OF LIFE FOR WHICH WE ALL HAVE ENORMOUS, INNATE POTENTIAL. SADLY THE POTENTIAL GOES BEGGING BECAUSE WE FAIL TO REALIZE THAT ONLY WE CAN DEVELOP IT. TO DEVELOP OUR POTENTIAL, WE MUST DEFINE THE QUALITIES, THE PRACTICED SKILLS, THAT MAKE A PERSON A LOVER; TAKE CAREFUL NOTICE OF THE IMPACT THAT LOVERS HAVE ON THEIR SURROUNDINGS; HELP PEOPLE LEARN HOW TO BE MORE EFFECTIVE

LOVERS; AND FIND NEW, POWERFUL WAYS OF PUTTING LOVE INTO PRACTICE.

ONCE WE BEGIN THIS, WE MAY DISCOVER NOT JUST WHAT LOVE WE ARE CAPABLE OF, BUT WHAT LOVE MAKES US CAPABLE OF.

WE MIGHT ALL ADMIT TO OURSELVES THAT LOVE REALLY IS THE ANSWER, THAT ONLY INDIVIDUALS CARING ABOUT EACH OTHER CAN AFFECT THIS WORLD. BUT AS SOON AS WE ADMIT THAT, OUR HARDENED SENSES OF REALITY TAKE HOLD AND SHAKE OFF SUCH WILD THOUGHTS, ADMONISHING US ABOUT INDULGING IN DREAMS.

AND AT LEAST FOR NOW THOSE THOUGHTS ARE DREAMS, FOR WE KNOW SO LITTLE ABOUT LOVE.

WE ARE INADEQUATE LOVERS, NOT PERMITTING OUR-SELVES TO DISCOVER AND DEVELOP ALL THE LOVE THERE IS, IN OURSELVES AND IN OTHERS. THIS BOOK IS TO HELP PEOPLE TAKE A STEP TOWARD BECOMING THE LOVERS THEY WERE BORN TO BE.

how to be a great lover

7IRST COMES

ABOUT YOURSELF. THE WORLD LOVES
A LOVER AND YOU ARE THE CENTER
OF YOUR WHOLE WORLD. YOU'VE GOT
TO LOVE YOURSELF.

NEXT COMES

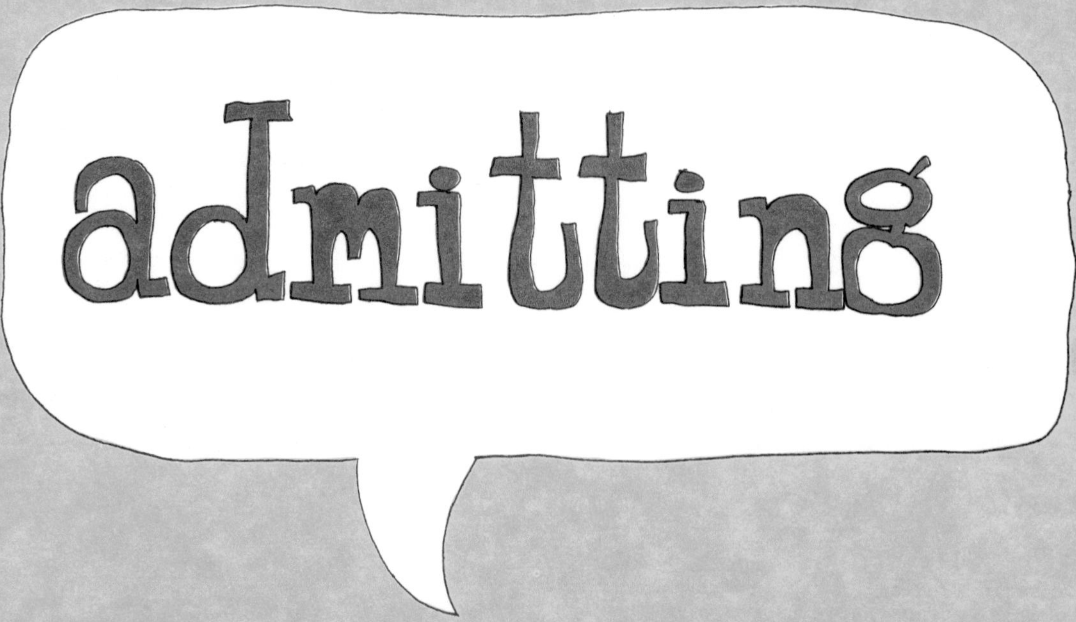
admitting

THAT YOU CARE, WHICH IS HARD BECAUSE
SOME PEOPLE DON'T LIKE IT WHEN YOU
CARE. BUT IF YOU CAN'T ADMIT THAT YOU
CARE, THEN NO ONE WILL EVER KNOW.
AND YOU WILL NEVER KNOW HOW MUCH YOU
CARE EITHER. BUT IF YOU WANT TO FIND
OUT, THEN YOU WILL BE

WilliNG

TO LISTEN TO THE VOICES INSIDE YOU. WHICH MEANS
LISTENING, NOT JUST WANTING TO. AND WHEN YOU
LISTEN, YOU FIND OUT WHAT YOU CARE ABOUT, WHICH
IS WHAT MAKES YOU, YOU.

IF YOU CARE ABOUT FRIENDS AND SECURITY, LIKE
SOME PEOPLE,

IF YOU CARE ABOUT SLIPCOVERS AND ARTICHOKE
HEARTS LIKE OTHER PEOPLE,

OR WHATEVER YOU CARE ABOUT
YOUR CARING WILL BE

IN ALL THE WORLD, BECAUSE THE WAY THAT YOU CARE WILL COME OUT OF YOU. AND THERE IS ONLY **1** OF YOU. ONLY YOU CAN CARE FOR THE WORLD AS YOU DO. ONLY YOU ARE CAPABLE OF CHANGING THIS WORLD WITH YOUR SPECIAL CARE.

NOW CARING AND ADMITTING HAVE LED A WILLING YOU TO YOUR OWN UNIQUENESS, WHICH CANNOT BE IGNORED. SO

BECAUSE THEN YOU WILL
BE ABLE TO SEE THE
UNIQUE,
MYSTERIOUS BEAUTY
OF
EVERY
HUMAN
PERSON

WHICH MEANS

RESPECTING

UNIQUENESS, ALLOWING AND ENCOURAGING
PEOPLE TO BE DIFFERENT FROM YOU.

A WORD TO THE WISE:
TO DO THIS, PERCEIVING PEOPLE
ACCURATELY, WITHOUT PRE-
JUDICIAL LABELS, IS A MUST.
THIS MEANS YOU CANNOT
FIT PEOPLE INTO YOUR MENTAL
IMAGES OF WHO YOU WANT
THEM TO BE.

AND SOON, WHEN YOUR WORLD IS FILLED
WITH WONDERFULLY DIFFERENT, UNIQUE
PEOPLE, YOU WILL FEEL LIKE

(AND YOU PROBABLY WILL SAY, "BOY, I SURE
AM GLAD THAT WE ARE ALL DIFFERENT!")

BUT THEN, BENEATH THE TUMULT OF YOUR REJOICING,
YOU WILL HEAR A LITTLE VOICE INSIDE YOU. IF YOU
LISTEN, YOU WILL HEAR AN ECHO FROM PLACES SO
DEEP INSIDE, THAT YOU DID NOT KNOW THEY WERE THERE.

AND MAYBE YOU WILL THINK, "BUT I HAVE JUST FOUND
SUCH A UNIQUE WORLD, WHY SHOULD I LEAVE?" BUT
THE ECHO CONTINUES AND WHEN IT IS VERY VERY
QUIET AROUND YOU, YOU WILL FIND YOURSELF

TO DISCOVER HOW MUCH MORE CARING YOU
ARE CAPABLE OF AND SO YOU WILL BEGIN
TO DIG DOWN AND EXPLORE THIS RICH VEIN OF
PRECIOUS TREASURES WITHIN YOU.

AS YOU FOLLOW ALONG THE PATHWAY YOU BEGIN

REALIZING

THAT THERE IS MORE TO YOU THAN YOU KNEW
(AND YOU WILL PROBABLY SAY, " HEY, I DIDN'T
KNOW ALL THIS STUFF WAS HERE. ")

AND SO YOU BEGIN

learning

WHAT THERE IS INSIDE YOU THAT LED YOU TO YOUR CARING AND YOUR UNIQUENESS. YOU COME TO KNOW YOURSELF AND YOUR ABILITIES. YOU SPEND TIME WITH YOURSELF, YOUR CARING.

YOU MAY BE ONE OF THE WORLD'S GREATEST WINKERS, CAPABLE OF BRINGING JOY TO MANY PEOPLE WITH YOUR WINK. BUT IF YOU DON'T KNOW THIS, ALL THAT WONDERFUL JOY MAY NEVER BE REALIZED.

IN THE MIDST OF ALL THIS MARVELOUS LEARNING, YOU ARE SURPRISED AT A LITTLE TWINGE OF PAIN THAT BOUNCES AROUND IN THE BACK OF YOUR MIND, THEN WORKS ITS WAY DOWN YOUR THROAT AND INTO YOUR STOMACH. YOU NOW REALIZE THAT BEING A GREAT LOVER DOESN'T COME EASY BECAUSE YOU KNOW THAT THE LITTLE TWINGE IS THE EMANCIPATED POTENTIAL OF YOUR CARING TRYING TO FIND ITS PLACE AMONG YOUR OLD HABITS AND DAILY ROUTINES. THOSE OLD WAYS DON'T WANT TO MOVE; THEY HAVE GOTTEN COMFORTABLE THERE. BUT YOUR NEW POTENTIAL NEEDS ROOM TO GROW, AND YOU HAVE TO FACE

WHAT TO DO WITH IT. IF YOU WAIT A LITTLE WHILE, IT WILL SLIP BACK INTO THE DARKNESS OF THE UNEXPLORED YOU, AND THE PAIN WILL GO WITH IT. THEN YOUR HABITS AND ROUTINES CAN RELAX AND GO ABOUT THEIR BUSINESS. AND YOU CAN GO BACK TO BEING WHO YOU WERE AND WHO YOU WILL BE.

BUT IF WHO YOU WERE WAS NOT WHO YOU WANT TO BE, THEN YOU BETTER DECIDE FAST, BECAUSE THAT POTENTIAL HAS ALREADY STARTED BACK DOWN. SO DECIDE, NOW, AND ASK YOURSELF

WHAT DO I WANT TO DO WITH MY LOVE? MY LIFE?

DO I WANT TO VISIT THE AGED?

DO I WANT TO NURSE THE SICK?

DO I WANT TO ADVANCE THE KNOWLEDGE OF SCIENCE?

DO I WANT TO FEED THE WORLD?

DO I WANT TO SERVE GOD?

DO I WANT TO TEACH CHILDREN?

DO I WANT TO CARE FOR STRAY DOGS?

DO I WANT TO CONSERVE THE EARTH?

DO I WANT TO MAKE BEAUTIFUL THINGS?

DO I WANT TO HAVE A GLORIOUS GARDEN?

DO I WANT TO CHANGE THE WORLD?

DO I WANT TO GROW?

DO I WANT TO CARE?

THESE ARE THE QUESTIONS THAT LOVERS ASK,
QUESTIONS ABOUT WHAT THEY WANT TO DO WITH
THEIR LIVES. BECAUSE THAT IS HOW LOVERS
DECIDE THEY CAN BEST LOVE. SO IF YOU DECIDE
TO BE A LOVER, YOU DECIDE HOW YOU ARE GOING
TO LOVE THE WORLD. AND WHEN YOU DECIDE THAT,
YOU BEGIN

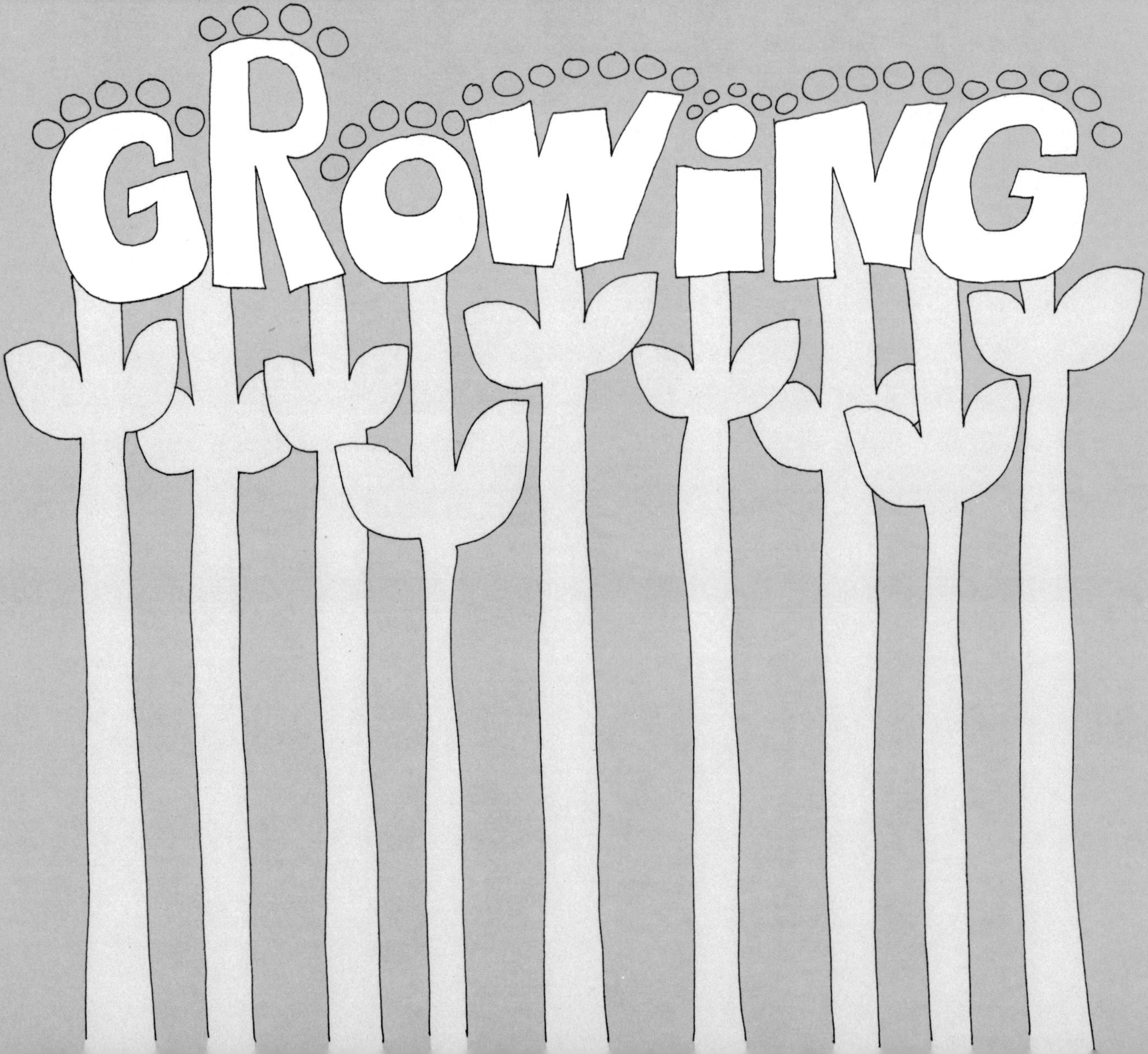
GROWING

AS YOU DEVELOP YOUR UNIQUENESS, AS YOU
FIND WAYS TO CHANGE YOUR WORLD WITH YOUR
LOVE, AS YOU MAKE A DIFFERENCE.

AND THEN YOU LOOK AROUND AND SEE THAT
YOU ARE

OUT YOUR LOVE, RICHLY, FULLY, WITH NO APOLOGIES
OR EXCUSES, WITH WONDERMENT AND FEELING AND
ZEST. AND YOU ARE ALWAYS LOVING, ALWAYS
BECOMING A GREATER LOVER. WHICH MEANS THAT
YOU ARE ALWAYS

TOUCHING

WHICH MEANS THAT WITH WORDS OR SMILES OR
HANDS OR ACTIONS THAT YOU ARE COMMUNICATING
YOUR LOVE; YOU CAN'T HELP TOUCHING PEOPLE WITH
YOUR LOVE BECAUSE EVERYTHING THAT A LOVER DOES
TOUCHES SOMEONE, SOMEHOW, SO YOU CAN ONLY
HOPE THAT IT WILL BE AS GOOD FOR OTHERS AS
IT IS FOR YOU. AND TOUCHING MEANS

being there

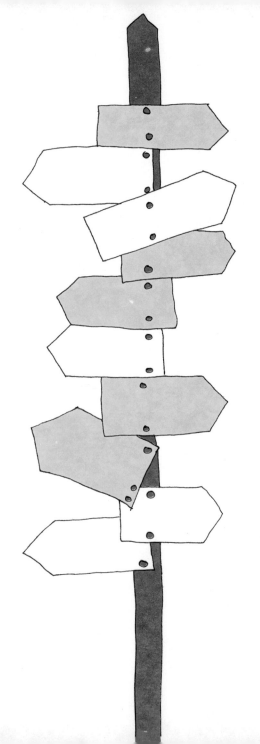

FOR OTHERS. IT MEANS THAT LOVERS ARE A PART OF OTHER LOVERS; INVOLVED; WRAPPED UP. AND SOMETIMES BEING THERE WRAPS YOU UP AND BEGINS TO SMOTHER YOU AND YOU HAVE TO PULL BACK, SENSING A LACK OF CONTROL AND FEARING THAT YOU'VE GONE TOO FAR, LOST YOURSELF, BEEN SWALLOWED UP. BUT STILL YOU KNOW THAT YOUR MOST PRECIOUS MOMENTS COME FROM BEING THERE, KNOWING THAT EVEN WHEN YOU CAN'T PHYSICALLY BE THERE, YOU ARE A PART OF SOMEONE'S LIFE.

AND GETTING THERE MEANS

GOING
OUT
07
YOUR
WAY

INCONVENIENCES ARE NOTHING BUT
OPPORTUNITIES THAT ASK A LITTLE
EXTRA EFFORT TO LOVE SOMEBODY.
YOU KNOW IT'S WORTH IT... BECAUSE
IT MAKES POSSIBLE

GIVING

NOT JUST WANTING TO GIVE, OR GIVING IN ORDER
TO GET, BUT GIVING, FREELY, NOT FROM WHAT IS
LEFTOVER, BUT FROM WHAT IS YOURS, WHAT IS
YOU.
SO IF MONEY IS YOU, GIVE MONEY.
IF YOU VALUE TIME, GIVE THAT.

BUT WHATEVER YOU GIVE, GIVE FROM THE HEART, FOR
A GIFT FROM YOUR HEART CAN BE GIVEN BY NO
OTHER. AND IT WILL STAY IN YOUR HEART
FOREVER.

MAYBE THIS, GIVING, IS WHAT IT ALL COMES DOWN
TO. BUT BEFORE GIVING, THERE IS

Receiving

WITH THE HONOR OF ONE WHO APPRECIATES FIRST
THE GIVER, THEN THE GIFT;
WITH THE GRACE OF ONE WHO THANKS THE GIVER FOR
THE LOVE THAT BROUGHT THE GIFT;
WITH THE DIGNITY OF ONE WHO RECEIVES FREELY, SO
THAT GIFTS MAY BE GIVEN FREELY.

ONCE YOU FREELY GIVE AND RECEIVE, YOU DISCOVER

Sharing

THE FLOW OF IDEAS AND EXPERIENCES AND ENERGIES BETWEEN PEOPLE THAT MAKES YOU'S AND THEY'S INTO WE'S; IT MEANS COMPETING SO THAT WE CAN GROW CLOSER TO EACH OTHER AND TO OURSELVES; IT MEANS COOPERATING SO THAT WE MAY KNOW THE WONDERS OF INDIVIDUALS WORKING TOGETHER; IT MEANS EXPRESSING YOUR NEEDS AND WANTS, YOUR DREAMS, YOUR HUMAN-NESS TO THOSE AROUND YOU, AND HELPING THEM FEEL BETTER ABOUT THEIR OWN; IT MEANS KNOWING THAT YOU WILL NEVER HAVE THOSE MOMENTS WITH THOSE PEOPLE AGAIN. AND IF YOU ARE EVER SHARING, THEN YOU ARE

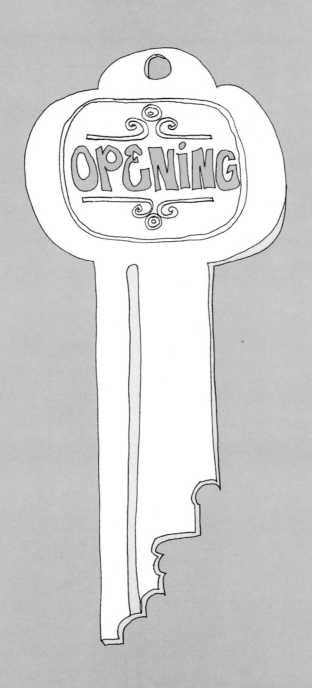

YOURSELF UP, LETTING PEOPLE KNOW YOU,
WHICH IS SCARY BECAUSE IT INVOLVES

RISKING

BEING VULNERABLE, TAKING A CHANCE ON LETTING
PEOPLE KNOW HOW HUMAN YOU ARE, ON BEING
ACCEPTED AND LOVED AND REJECTED AND HURT.
BUT THERE IS A GREAT SAFETY IN KNOWING THAT
YOU ARE THE ONLY ONE WHO CAN OPEN YOU UP, AND THE
ONLY ONE WHO CAN TAKE YOUR UNIQUENESS AND
MAKE YOU A TRULY UNIQUE LOVER.

DOING THIS REQUIRES
            CONSTANT,
            AND EVER SO GENTLE,

PUSHING

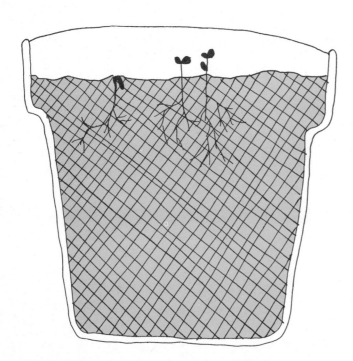

TO FIND YOUR OWN LIMITS, TO DISCOVER WHAT AND
TO WHOM YOU CAN OPENLY ADMIT YOUR UNIQUENESS,
TO EXERCISE YOUR ABILITY TO LOVE. AND THIS GENTLE
PUSHING, DONE WITH GREAT CARE BECAUSE OF THE
SENSITIVE NATURE OF LOVERS, WILL LEAD YOU TO
EXPERIENCE THE MAGNIFICENT CONFIDENCE OF

trusting

WHICH IS THE FOUNDATION, BUILT BY HAND,
PATIENTLY AND CAREFULLY,
OF MEANING IN ANY RELATIONSHIP.

ALLOWING YOURSELF
TO BE TRUSTED,
AND TO TRUST OTHERS,
MEANS THAT YOU ARE

OF THE MEANING THAT LOVE BRINGS TO YOUR LIFE,
OF WHAT IT TAKES TO BE A LOVER,
OF YOUR ENDLESS BECOMING,
OF YOUR OWN UNIQUENESS,
OF YOUR POTENTIAL FOR

WHICH MEANS WE ARE RIGHT BACK
WHERE WE STARTED, WHICH IS WHAT
LOVE IS ALL ABOUT.